THE
BRIDE

ZABEL
ASADOUR

Translated By

NISHAN PARLAKIAN

A GRIFFON HOUSE PUBLICATION

Library of Congree Cataloging-in-Publication Data

Asatur, Zapel, 1863-1934.
　　The bride　:　a play.

　　Translation of: Harse.
　　[Trans. by Nishan Parlakian]
　　I.　Title.
PK8548.A838H3713　　1987　　891' .99225　　87-12036
ISBN 0-918680-37-9

ISBN: 0-918680-37-9
GHD 902

Published by

GRIFFON HOUSE PUBLICATIONS
P. O. Box 81, Whitestone New York 11357

CONTENTS

TO *MY* BRIDE, FLO —

This publication of the first English translation of THE BRIDE *was made possible in part by grants from the Alex Manoogian Cultural Fund of the Armenian General Benevolent Union (with the cooperation of Mr. Edmund Y. Azadian), The Walter Bagehot Research Council, and the Council on National Literatures, whose member libraries (in over 40 foreign countries) will receive copies of the volume as a generous "bonus."*

ACKNOWLEDGEMENTS

There are many people who deserve to be remembered here for their support and encouragement, but I will have to limit myself to only a few: His Eminence Archbishop Torkom Manoogian, Primate of the Diocese of the Armenian Church of America; Mr. Michael Kermian, former Director of the Diocese; and the members of the Auxiliary Committee, —all of whom were instrumental in making possible the original production of *The Bride* in Armenian in November 1984 at the Kavookjian Auditorium at the Diocese. That production was given memorable form by the excellent acting of Harout Tirakian, Elizabeth Khodabash, Roubina Mamalian, and Lucyn Jamgotchian; the lovely authentic turn-of-the-century costumes created by Magradel Hicks; and by the fine photographs of the well known H. Kantzabed—several of which have been included in this volume and one of which is featured on the cover.

I wish also to thank the readers of my English translation of the play (1986): Rita Brodley (who also served as director), Joseph V. Francis, Jackie Brodley, Judy Victor, and Ann Mounti.

A very special debt of gratitude is due Dr. Marzbed Margossian, noted writer and translator, who solved for me the meaning of a proverb rendered in the original text in a non-Armenian language.

To my good friend and colleague, Dr. Anne Paolucci of St. John's University, my continuing gratitude for her constant interest in things Armenian and especially, in this case, for her efforts in getting the translation published, for supervising the manuscript along the way, and for agreeing so graciously to write an "Afterword" for this book.

N.P.
May 1987

Zabel Asadour, author of *The Bride.* From a photograph
reproduced in *Sipil: Zapel Asatur,* Erevani Hamalsarani
Hratakch'ut'yun, 1980.

Zabel Asadour (Khanjian), *born on July 23, 1863 in Scutari [a suburb of Constantinople], is regarded as a leading Anatolian-Armenian woman writer—a poet, novelist, and journalist. Early in her career, she wrote for Constantinople newspapers under the pseudonyms of "Sybil" and "Miss Alice." In 1879, barely sixteen, she formed with eight school friends the National Armenian Women's Union, a group which was instrumental in establishing schools and orphanages in rural areas—a blessing for poor girls in the provinces. (In 1915, when national disaster struck, the progressive work of the Union came to an end.) Mrs. Asadour was deeply committed to the cause of education and became one of Constantinople's pre-eminent teachers. With her husband, Hrand Asadour, she prepared a series of educational readers, including* Museums *and* The New Armenian Grammar. *A professional writer, her essentially literary works, published from time to time, included novels (e.g.* A Girl's Heart)*, a collection of short stories (*Women's Souls)*, and a volume of poetry (*Reflections)*. The Constantinople community was about to celebrate the fifieth year of this talented writer's contribution to literature and public service when unfortunately her fruitful life came to an end on June 19, 1934.*

[Translated from the 1938 Armenian Edition of *The Bride (Harsub)*, which was published by Hairenik Press (Boston).

ՄԱՏԵՆԱՇԱՐ «ԱՐՄԵՆԻԱ» ԹԻՒ 1

ՋԱՊԷԼ ԱՍԱՏՈՒՐ
(ՍԻՊԻԼ)

ՀԱՐՍԸ

ՏՊԱՐԱՆ «ՀԱՅՐԵՆԻՔ»Ի
ՊՈՍԹՐՆ
1938

Reproduction of the cover of the Armenian edition of
The Bride: 1938, Hairenik Press, Boston.

ՄԱՏԵՆԱՇԱՐ «ԱՐՄԵՆԻԱ» Թիւ 1

ԶԱՊԷԼ ԱՍԱՏՈՒՐ
(ՍԻՊԻԼ)

ՀԱՐՍԸ

Պ Ո Ս Տ Ո Ն
1938

Reproduction of the title page of the Armenian edition
of *The Bride*: 1938, Hairenik Press, Boston.

TRANSLATOR'S PREFACE

Relatively few in numbers and spread out, over the centuries, across the Anatolian peninsula, from the Caucasus mountains in the East to the Bosporos straits on the verge of Europe in the West, Armenians nevertheless have maintained a strong sense of national and cultural unity and produced notable works of art. In the middle ages they excelled in illuminated manuscripts and built impressive and architecturally unique churches; later, religiously inspired art gave way to original works and others in translation, culminating—in the modern age—in the creation of the most significant new drama of the Near East, with major centers of theatrical activity in Tiflis and Constantinople.

In the East, Gabriel Sundukian (1815-1912)—perhaps the greatest of all Armenian dramatists—wrote bitter-sweet plays like *Bebo* and *Khatabala*. His *Ruined Family*, rich in comedic overtones, has been likened to the social plays of Ibsen.[1] But closer to the sober realistic social consciousness of Ibsen are the plays of Alexandre Shirvanzade (1858-1935), another Eastern Armenian writer based in Baku and Tiflis. Shirvanzade is said to be the originator of modern Armenian drama with such strong plays as *For the Sake of Honor* and *Evil Spirit.* The tone and quality of his works take us into the early part of the twentieth century, especially a play like *Did She Have the Right?* with its feminist implications, which suggest direct borrowings from Ibsen's *Doll House.*

Perhaps the most seminal dramatic influence in Western Anatolia—Constantinople specifically—were the works of Hagop Baronian (1842-1891). Although scholars like Krikor Maksudian correctly note that Baronian did not actually write plays, the consensus of opinion is that his prose satires, reminiscent of Molière in their portrayal of the foibles and follies of middle-class Armenian society, are inherently dramatic and readily adaptable for the stage. Asadour's *The Bride*, translated in this volume, suggests Baronian's style in many ways and explores two of his themes:

10

one is the putative argument that the big city—in this case Constantinople—is the ostensible model of good breeding; the other is that women should not venture beyond the rigorous limits defined by a paternalistic society.

The first theme is developed through comic and satiric exchanges to underscore the cliché that country folk and small town people are common and vulgar, often taken advantage of by those more clever than they. Baronian had ably portrayed in the *Gentlemen Beggars* the human leeches of Constantinople, who try to suck money out of the pockets of those from the Anatolian "interior." So too in *The Bride*: Arousiag, the newly-married girl from the country, is looked down on by her middle-class mother-in-law and sister-in-law as socially inferior. The plot takes on more complex turns as the reader discovers with Arousiag the dishonesty and hypocrisy of her self-ordained "superior" in-laws.

Asadour's treatment of women in *The Bride* suggests something of the aggressiveness of Baronian's *Brother Balthazar,* in which a woman arrogantly gives vent to her adulterous designs to the utter chagrin of her sad and hapless husband, and the relentless efforts of the wife in *The Eastern Dentist* to track down and expose her husband's adulterous adventures. But Baronian's treatment of these two themes is harshly direct: the women in both plays are hardened and seasoned wives who win out by asserting themselves boldly, unyielding in their purpose. In Asadour's *The Bride*, Arousiag also wins out, but by other means. Arousiag, loses none of her innocence and purity in the end; she remains the dutiful loving wife who is forced to uphold what is right, even if her in-laws have to be unmasked. She is as honorable as Markarid, the heroine in Shirvanzade's *For the Sake of Honor*; she is patient, clever, resourceful, idealistic in her love for her husband; she embodies a distinctive new quality that is not revolt in the gross sense but large understanding which she is able to turn to her advantage in the battle for place and respect. What is interesting about this play, also, is the fact that Asadour depicts a marriage of love not convenience. Moreover, Arousiag remains true to her good instincts even after she has revealed the hypocrisy and greed of her mother-

11

in-law and sister-in-law. She has not been spoiled by the experience. It has served only to strengthen her bond with her husband, who accepts her values and stands by her. In its strong appeal to equal respect and dignity for women and to love-marriages, *The Bride* emerges as the first modern romantic play in the Armenian repertory, far ahead of its time.

It would not be far fetched to say that in her writings Asadour drew from her own marriage and her experience in advancing women's causes. Throughout her life she remained a keen observer of the condition and place of women in Armenian society. Married at eighteen to Garabed Donelian, a lawyer, she accompanied him into the hinterlands and small towns of Anatolia to set up schools expressly for the education of young girls. She contributed to periodicals in Constantinople and later wrote about women in novels and stories such as *A Girl's Heart* and *Women's Souls* under the pseudonym of "Sybil."

Although the word itself may not have been in vogue yet in her time and place, later observers have in fact called Asadour an "ardent feminist."[2] A. M. Minasian notes that after the death of her first husband and her marriage to the noted writer Hrand Asadour, "Sybil" became "committed to women's rights" and "hoped that Armenian women would be able, even in a small way, to share in the progressive European women's movement."[3] Still, *The Bride* does not represent, as already noted, a "feminist" tract in the manner of Shirvanzade's *Did She Have the Right?* Asadour's play explores the boundaries of a wife's rights as a human being, calling for proper respect and honor—especially in the kind of home situation most Armenian brides found themselves in at the turn of the century, where the mother-in-law ruled the household and her family came first in all things—husbands too, very often, siding with their mothers against their wives. In Asadour's play the situation is depicted clearly and realistically but without the strident quality of Baronian's works or the forceful dramatization of women's prerogatives in Shirvanzade.

Asadour seems to have moved easily from the narrative to the dramatic form. Unlike Baronian, who seems

12

to have been first and foremost a satirist prose writer and whose "plays" are loaded with narrative passages perhaps left over from his original prose writings, Asadour seems to have gravitated naturally to the dramatic form from prose writing. One of her fictional works, *True Feminism,* was a narrative in a three-act near-play form. By 1909 however she had written a play called *The Magnis* in the foreword of which she asked interested young women to stage the work. In the wake of these narrative-dramatic expressions of feminist ideas, *The Bride* should not surprise us. What is surprising is the way in which Asadour manages to retain such things as Baronian's long monologues without destroying the easy balance of dramatic elements in her play. Toward the end, especially, the monologue becomes vitally dramatic as we "overhear" the conflicting plots, doubts, and innermost feelings of the characters. The comedy which results from the clever juxtaposition of such monologues is effective, in the style of the "Absurd" rather than the "well made play" of the nineteenth century.

The comic thread that runs through this play is perhaps its most interesting feature and softens, with "distance," what could easily have become a "women's lib" tirade. Asadour justifiably asserts a wife's priorities, but never oversteps the bounds of propriety. She does not destroy the rights of others: others destroy themselves by lying and cheating. She is truly self-sacrificing, putting her husband's well-being above her own in all things. She upholds the ideal of love in marriage and allows her husband to retain his dignity even as the unscrupulous intentions of his own mother and sister are brought to light. She never presses her advantage and never takes the offensive in the confrontations instigated by her in-laws. In short: the play makes a strong statement for its time but does not undermine traditional values in so doing; it simply expands the horizons and prepares the world stage for a new kind of voice.

Sacrificing the neat plot that works to a predictable conclusion in the tradition of the well-made play, Asadour brings the work to an abrupt ending in which the guilty are unmasked, the good glorified, but the final resolution and restoration of balance is left an open question. This quick ending, seen in the total context of a new stage language, still not fully articulated, works well on stage: the monologues have a frenetic agitated quality that is reminscent of certain passages in Ionesco and Pinter. In its first performance in English, at the reading held on June 9, 1986 at the Diocese of the Armenian Church in New York City, the actors gave theatrical immediacy to a situation that could easily have deteriorated into bathos. The wife who sacrifices all her worldly treasures to save her husband from alleged bank-ruptcy, a husband who struggles against the realization that his sister is stealing from him for her own ends and his mother is plotting against his wife, who must carry his own plans to their inevitable conclusion in order to restore his wife to her rightful place and prove her true and loyal, a sister and mother who seem to have no redeeming qualities whatsoever:—such characters must be given dramatic scope to succeed on stage. Perhaps Asadour was too close to what she was depicting to match the satiric detachment of Molière. But the play has its own stride and inner cohesiveness. Certainly it must be read within the context of the cultural and sociological realities of the time, but whatever its shortcomings stylistically it is a powerful statement, a provocative "first," a new kind of drama. Its strength lies in its unwavering commitment to a basic human principle.

What ultimately wins out is love—an emotion that is suspect in a society where marriages are arranged and are very often economic transactions. Mrs. Dirouhi is critical of Arousiag's romantic attitude toward marriage, her often-repeated "I love Arshag." The older woman comments: "I've been married too and looked after a husband. Did I ever utter such shameless words?" Arousiag's uninhibited manner is obviously wrong. "What really gets on my nerves is her constant singing. She never lets up. She sings as she straightens up, she sings when she sews, she sings when she makes the beds. She sings, sings, sings. What must the neighbors think. They must think we run a night club here, 'Cafe Chantons.' And another thing. I can't stand her going off to her room to write. There's no end to it. She writes in the morning. She writes

at night:— What is she writing?" Arousiag is writing, of all
things, a love story! When she reads part of it to her sister-
in-law, Hanumig tells her mother: "I covered my ears, Momma. I told her I didn't want to hear such things."

"Such things" are not proper. Good girls hem,
embroider, stay home and do the chores they are told to do,
and when they venture out they do so under carefully pre-
scribed conditions. They certainly don't go running off by
themselves, visiting friends and museums; a well brought up
girl—married or unmarried—doesn't make a spectacle of
herself. Arousiag doesn't even pretend to be interested in
hemming handkerchiefs and she does not offer to help her
sister-in-law in that task. There is a touch of envy as well as
self-righteous smugness in Hanumig's complaints: "Who
needs her or her hemming. I wouldn't let her touch the work.
It's just that she ought to offer to help at least once in a
while. One ought to ask, at least once, out of courtesy." Her
insistence on formalities, proprieties, social clichés, and
stifling patterns of behavior suggests (among other things)
ambivalent feelings: the unmarried girl who recognizes in her
brother's young wife an assertive personality and yet is afraid
to acknowledge its attraction openly. Hanumig has her
own petty plans for advancing her place in society, but true
to the hypocrisy encouraged by all the rigorous formalities of
right and wrong behavior, she hides them from the world,
plotting the worst kind of fraud on her brother and his wife
even as she criticizes their behavior. It is Arousiag who
punctures the vanity and empty rhetoric of her in-laws. In
her genuine affection for her husband, in her good-natured
efforts to translate the criticism of her in-laws into neutral
terms and keep a cheerful disposition throughout, in her
willingness to sell her jewelry to raise money for her husband—appealing, with a certain business acumen, even to her
own people for help in a way that would not undermine
Arshag's integrity as the head of the household—Arousiag is
like a breath of fresh air in a closed and stuffy room. She
represents spontaneity and honesty in a world where the
weight of the neighbor's silver is cause for brooding and envy,
where the trappings of bourgeois comforts are the measure of

15

status and importance, where following conventions unquestioningly is the standard of goodness, where silent brooding is mistaken for modesty.

Asadour is indeed claiming a new independence for women, but she wins her battle without disrupting the basic fibre of family values or disrupting the relationships on which those values rest. If Hanumig suffers in the end, it is something she has brought upon herself. Arousiag is not out for vengeance; she remains herself, and her faith and loyalty are unblemished. In her husband's love and trust is her victory. What happens to the guilty is not her concern: she has simply stumbled on a plot that in her eyes threatened her husband and had to be stopped for the sake of everything that is right and good. She allows the facts to come to light but only when she is forced to protect herself.

In his role as son, brother and husband, Arshag tries his best to live within the rigorously-defined relationships of Armenian society: a mother should be honored at all times, a sister should be protected and properly cared for and a good marriage arranged for her in due course, a wife should be chosen so that there is harmony in the household; but even before the melodramatic revelation at the end of the play, Arshag has given ample proof of his loyalty to his wife and the choice he ultimately makes is in her favor. Asadour has caught all the particulars and flavor of a period piece that is also a historical statement, a moment of transition. *The Bride* may not satisfy some of our current tastes: most women are not expected to move in with their in-laws and take a modest second or third place in the household; and marriages are not negotiated with formal matchmakers preparing formal contracts to be signed by both parties. Social realities and social taboos are always changing. Yet, even within a historical context that may no longer be compelling to us today, *The Bride* has its own unembellished charm; its language sometimes may lack subtlety, but it never falters; its ending is properly exaggerated in favor of one side to offset the exaggerated claims of the other. Perhaps it is more correctly a dramatic statement inspired by a zealous cause. Whatever the final judgment, it is clearly a play worth

16

reading and performing. And well worth translating.

NOTES

1.   See the Introduction by Robert Arnot to "Armenian Literature" (p. vii) in *The World's Great Classics,* The Colonial Press, New York and London, 1901. The volume also contains a complete book-length section entitled "Babylonian and Assyrian Literature."

2.   See *The Armenian Mirror,* Boston, July 31, 1934, p. 3.

3.   See *Sipil: Zapel Asatur,* Erevani Hamalsarani Hratakch'ut'yun, 1980, pp. 6 and 7.

[The translation that follows is from the 1938 Armenian edition of the play published by Hairenik Press, Boston.]

****

CHARACTERS

ARSHAG ARDZATIAN *(a young businessman)*
MRS. DIROUHI *(his mother)*
MISS HANUMIG *(his sister)*
AROUSIAG *(his young wife)*
A MAID

[The action takes place in the sitting room of the Ardzatian family home in Constantinople, at the turn of the century.]

Roubina Mamalian as Arousiag (left) and Elizabeth Khodabashian as Mrs. Dirouhi (right) in the Armenian production of *The Bride* (November 1984, New York).

Harout Tirakian as Arshag (left) and Roubina Mamalian
as Arousiag (right).

Lucyn Jamgotchian as Hanumig (left) and Roubina
Mamalian as Arousiag (right).

Lucyn Jamgotchian as Hanumig (left) and Elizabeth Khodabashian as Mrs. Dirouhi (right).

Harout Tirakian as Arshag (left) and Elizabeth Khodabashian as Mrs. Dirouhi.

The full cast and director/translator of *The Bride*, following the New York City production, November 1984. From left to right: Harout Tirakian (Arshag), Roubina Mamalian (Arousiag), Lucyn Jamgotchian (Hanumig), Elizabeth Khodabashian (Mrs. Dirouhi), and Dr. Nishan Parlakian who directed the play and whose translation appears in this volume.

SCENE 1

(Mrs. Dirouhi and Hanumig)

MRS. DIROUHI

You've tired yourself, Hanumig. Put your work aside for a while, come here, look at all those people returning from the shore. Relax a bit. Open up your heart.

HANUMIG

Open up what heart? Do I have a heart left in me? I don't see anything that pleases me. I live in a dark narrow world. I feel I'm stifling every time I think about that outsider who has come into our home and wants to take over everything. I'm going mad. Not only has she taken my brother from me, she wants to take you away from me too. "Mother," she says. "Our house, our parlor," she says. The other day when we paid the Santigians a visit? They served us a glorious tea on their best china. I have to tell you, I couldn't get it out of my head, all the way home in the carriage. I was so upset, I couldn't bring myself to talk about it. "What's the matter," she asked me. "Their silver is so much heavier than ours," I said. Do you know what her answer was? "Ours is lovelier." The nerve. I was so put out I could have slapped her. Does she really think that what is ours is hers or that she has a right to any of it? I felt so awful that I went to my room and cried the rest of the day. I won't allow her to have a single thing in this house, not the smallest thing of ours! *(She wipes her eyes with a handkerchief.)*

MRS. DIROUHI

Don't be a baby, Hanumig dear. Aren't you ashamed crying like that? Who is she, what right does she have to anything? Whatever we own I will leave to you in my will so no one else can get at our things after my death. Right now what's on my mind is getting you married. We may have to sell the house in the country. Whatever we get from it will be turned over to you. She can sweet talk me all she wants—call me "Mother" and "Momma"—I'll never call her mine. A daughter-in-law is not one's flesh and blood. She's an outsider, an enemy!

24

HANUMIG

Tell that to Arshag. He's crazy about her. He gives her the carriage to drive in wherever she wants to go. And you haven't said a word about it. You're as soft as cotton. Where do you suppose she is this very minute? You used to criticize everything I did. You were always angry with me. What's happened to that big voice of yours? Yell and shout at her so she'll calm down. This house needs a voice of authority. Arshag is to blame. Did he ever bring us gifts? Now, every evening, he comes home with big packages.

MRS. DIROUHI

No, don't say that, Hanumig. Whatever he brings her they both share with you. Only the other day, he told you to choose from two *crêpe de chine* blouses. If the pair of them didn't treat you fairly, I'd bring the house down on their heads.

HANUMIG

I know how you bring down the house—with words! You're all talk! You never really do anything. If you had any real power around here you wouldn't let her laugh and chat with everyone who comes and goes, or let her wear those low-cut dresses or play the piano or sing for anyone who happens to come by. She does whatever you ask her to do so you'll like her. What about me? I'm only an old piece of luggage left in the corner. Am I the daughter of this house or is she?

MRS. DIROUHI

You're right. I've got to talk to Arshag. When he hears the things you've told me he'll put a stop to her shenanigans, you'll see. A married woman putting herself on display in front of strangers!!? Doing things that young girls like you have a right to do, not her. What really gets on my nerves is her constant singing. She never lets up. She sings as she straightens up, she sings when she sews, she sings when she makes the beds. She sings, sings, sings. What must the neighbors think? They must think we run a night club here, "Cafe Chantons." And another thing. I can't stand her going off to her room to write. There's no end to it. She writes in the morning. She writes at night:—What is she writing?

HANUMIG

Novels.

MRS. DIROUHI

What kind of novels?

HANUMIG

She makes up stories about this person, that one—

MRS. DIROUHI

I knew she made things up! Who does she write about? Have you seen any of it?

HANUMIG

She read me some the other day. Scandalous things. All about love. She has no sense of shame.

MRS. DIROUHI

I know, I know. She's got love on her brain. "I love Arshag," she says whenever she feels like saying it. Just like that, right in front of me. I've been married too and looked after a husband. Did I ever utter such shameless words? How could she read such brazen things to you? Doesn't she realize that you're a proper, well-brought up young lady? By the way, what did you do when she read to you?

HANUMIG

I covered my ears, Momma. I told her I didn't want to hear such things. I ran out of the room, I was so angry.

MRS. DIROUHI

I've got to talk to Arshag. If she can write romantic novels, she can also write love letters . . . .

HANUMIG

The same thought crossed my mind. But when are you going

to find a moment to speak with Arshag privately? She doesn't leave him for a second.

MRS. DIROUHI

That's what you think. She lies around in the morning doing nothing. What I'll do is get up at dawn and wait for Arshag to come downstairs. That's when I'll straighten him out. I'll tell him all about her eccentric behavior. Men are like weather vanes. They turn whichever way the wind blows. Once he realizes that we're right, mark my words, he'll cool towards her. And once he stops fueling her oven, she'll grow cool and so will we. Then we'll take Arshag in hand. We'll coax him, convince him, persuade him to do exactly what we tell him to.

HANUMIG

I don't think she takes him seriously any more. We can knock her from morning till night, it won't have any effect on her. She'll turn everything into a joke and laugh. Shameless, that's what she is. Look: she sees I'm trying to finish these napkins as quickly as possible and I've only hemmed six of the twelve borders. You'd think she would do one or two of them herself, but no.

MRS. DIROUHI

Would you really trust her with that work? Do you think she can hem as well as you?

HANUMIG

Who needs her hemming! I wouldn't let her touch the work. It's just that she should at least once offer to help. Even just as a matter of form, a person should ask just once at least. When we run into people don't we tell them they are our best friends and are always welcome at our house? We lie a little out of courtesy.

MRS. DIROUHI

She doesn't know anything about the delicate art of hemming. She's a peasant. The other evening, the night of the

27

dance, she could have asked me to go along with the rest of you? You said it ten times if you said it once: "Momma, you should come with us." But she didn't open her mouth once. Not that I wanted to go, mind you. When I hinted to Arshag that she had hurt my feelings, he said, "Momma, Arousiag is not a hypocrite. She knows you don't go to dances. Why should she ask you silly questions?"

HANUMIG

She doesn't ask because she doesn't want to take the chance she'll be seen with us. To tell you the truth, I can't think of a reason for going anywhere with her myself. She likes to go places so that people will notice her. When you speak to Arshag, tell him I don't want to be seen with her. If he wants to take me anywhere, he'll have to take me alone. I'd rather sit home from now on and die of boredom than be seen with her. It's her fault that people are gossiping about us. She's ruining our good name.

MRS. DIROUHI

My dear child, don't you know your reputation is as precious as gold? Doesn't everybody know who you are? Who would ever gossip about you? The moment they tried anything like that they would be forced to shut up.

HANUMIG

Before we know it, we won't have a reputation to speak of. If people see the two of us in the same place, with Arshag, how can they tell his wife from his sister?

MRS. DIROUHI

Those who know, know; and those who don't, will ask. You are so different, why there's no comparison. First of all, you're built more delicately, you're smaller, you have a tiny waist and blue eyes. And with your golden hair you look like a little French Miss. She's nothing but a country bumpkin when all is said and done.

HANUMIG

She *is* tall, Momma.

MRS. DIROUHI

Ha! So is the pole at the end of the clothes line. I wonder how I can get Arshag to listen to me, now, after he went off and got married without my permission. Oh, I wish he hadn't had to go off like that. I'd never have allowed him to marry. When it was all over, I kept my mouth shut because of the dowry. Three thousand gold pieces! If not for that, what was the hurry? Was this the right time for him to get married? He should have settled you first! God willing, we'll come into some good luck soon. You won't have to live in this house with them for much longer.

HANUMIG

I couldn't stand it. It's impossible so long as Arousiag is in our house. She'll always push herself forward so no one will notice me. If you really want me to be happy, Momma, just pray that they quarrel and that Arousiag leaves him. Then we can live comfortably again, the way we used to. Haven't you noticed that since *she* set foot in this house I haven't been able to do a stitch of embroidery?

MRS. DIROUHI

My dear child, why? Don't let her presence bother you. Don't pay attention to anything she says or does. If you like, we'll spend our time in your room from now on and see her only at meals.

HANUMIG

Oh, if only you had arranged it that way at the very beginning . . . . We should have done that the first day she set foot in this house. Now we'll have to find a reason.

MRS. DIROUHI

We'll think up something. Don't worry, dear. Why should a new bride make you uneasy. You're in charge here from now on. I'm too old for the job. You're going to take my place. You'll be in total command. Tell me whenever anything displeases you. I really mean it. I'll have everything done to your liking.

HANUMIG
Oh, Momma! If you could just work things out so Arousiag would pack up and leave this house.

MRS. DIROUHI
I can do that easily enough, but I'm afraid Arshag would go after her. Then everything will get turned upside again. We might have to leave and find rooms elsewhere. We'd be forced to spend our own money. Now, even before paying the household bills, we're able to put away in the bank a good part of the money Arshag gives us. It would be better to keep his wife under our thumb here and use her as we wish. Let's try to find some way to prevent her from seeing our guests and going visiting with us.

HANUMIG
That won't do it. Arshag still has her expenses to cover. She'll still be eating into our household money. We've got to figure out a way to separate her from us completely.

MRS. DIROUHI
We'll find a way, dear. God willing, we'll manage that too. Patience. You know what patience means. It takes patience to turn grape into halva and mulberry leaves into silk.

SCENE 2
(Arousiag, Hanumig, Mrs. Dirouhi)

AROUSIAG
Hello, Momma. Hello, Hanumig. Still working?

HANUMIG
What, then? Somebody's got to work.

MRS. DIROUHI

30

That's right! We can't all go calling on people.

HANUMIG
If everybody went out to pay calls all day long, the house would fall apart.

AROUSIAG
Really? Do you think things would fall apart if you didn't get your hemming done? (*She takes off her hat and gloves and puts them down on the table.*)

HANUMIG
Are you making fun of me? That does it! You go to the cinema and to the theater while I stay here and work from dawn to dusk keeping the house clean and neat! And still you have the nerve to laugh at me.

AROUSIAG
What do you want me to say? Your hard work keeps the house from falling apart . . . ? My dear Hanumig, you seem a bit out of sorts again today. Let's go up to the terrace on the roof. The fresh air will do your nerves some good.

MRS. DIROUHI
Stop all this crowing. You sound like two old women arguing. Where do you think you are, in the Anatolian mountains? Anyone happening by our house would think there was a riot going on in here. Arousiag, my daughter is not the type who needs cooling off on the terrace. You should know better than to suggest such a thing. Mind what I say or you will suffer the consequences.

AROUSIAG
I always mind what you say, Momma. Haven't I always—?

MRS. DIROUHI
(*Interrupts*) Who do you ever listen to that you should suddenly listen to me? You're too independent.

AROUSIAG

You may be right. But with time and experience, I'll learn. After all, I was married right after I had finished school.

MRS. DIROUHI

You couldn't have been just out of school! You're certainly older than Hanumig.

AROUSIAG

Maybe. But age is not the issue. What I'm saying is that I spent very little time living among my family and friends.

MRS. DIROUHI

You couldn't have learned much from family or friends in the Anatolian mountains, could you?

AROUSIAG

The city of Smyrna is not exactly the Anatolian mountains, Momma. It's a city just like this one. And furthermore, as you know, my parents are Constantinopilites, originally—

MRS. DIROUHI

There are Constantinopilites and Constantinopilites. There are the upper classes like us and . . . there are . . . the others.

AROUSIAG

(Aside) She's at it again! I'll put a stop to it. (Aloud) You have a point. *Il y a cordonnier et cordonnier.*

HANUMIG

How dare you insult us, Arousiag! The idea of calling us shoemakers. You're too much!

AROUSIAG

You're much too sensitive. I was just quoting a French saying, only in jest.

HANUMIG

How's this for a saying: If you can't learn to speak pleasantly, learn to shut your mouth. You'd do well not to speak at all in this house. I'm going to my room, Momma. *(She takes up her work.)*

AROUSIAG

Don't fret on my account, Hanumig. I was just going upstairs to change for dinner anyway. *(She takes two steps toward the door.)*

MRS. DIROUHI

(Aside) Why change? Who is going to look at you? *(Aloud)* Take your hat with you. You need a maid to pick up after you. *(She hands her the hat.)*

AROUSIAG

Thank you, Momma. *(She takes the hat.)*

HANUMIG

(Sarcastically) Look, Momma, she's left her gloves here, too.

AROUSIAG

(She turns and takes up the gloves.) Excuse me.

HANUMIG

For everything? *(Continues as Arousiag leaves)* Sloppy slut. Oh, my poor brother! *(Arousiag exits through the door on the right.)*

SCENE 3
(Arshag, Mrs. Dirouhi, Hanumig)

ARSHAG

Good evening. *(Irritated, he takes off his hat, puts it on the table; Mrs. Dirouhi and Hanumig rise and go to stand on either side of him.)*

MRS. DIROUHI

Good evening, son.

HANUMIG

Do you want to take off your coat? Would you like your slippers? (*Arshag shakes his head.*)

MRS. DIROUHI

Come sit by me. Let me look at you. Are you feeling all right?

ARSHAG

(*Still ill-tempered*) Can't complain. Where's Arousiag?

MRS. DIROUHI

Ha! The first thing out of your mouth is about her! You don't ask about us, how *we* are—

ARSHAG

Why, have you been ill, Momma?

MRS. DIROUHI

Have I! I had a toothache all night long. I didn't close my eyes at all.

ARSHAG

You should have put some iodine on the tooth.

MRS. DIROUHI

Hanumig has one of her headaches again.

HANUMIG

Please, let's not talk about it. I'm not a sensitive delicate little creature. I can cope with pain. I don't expect anyone else to worry about it. I'm not the kind of person who wants the whole world to know when she's got a little pain in her pinky!

MRS. DIROUHI

(*Angry*) Don't say that! Don't ever say no one should worry! In my house everyone must worry for you, look after you. And anyone who doesn't is no child of mine.

34

ARSHAG

(Aside) Oh. Oh. They've started up the old routine again. *(Aloud)* Momma, I don't think I've shirked my obligations. What do you want of me? I come home tired. From sunrise to sunset I'm up to my ears in irritating problems. I have to deal with all sorts of business matters, both physically and morally demanding. What else should a breadwinner do? Take care of the house, coddle you all? I look after you to the best of my ability, I think. What about you? Are you concerned with my well-being?

HANUMIG

You don't need us. You've got a wife, now.

ARSHAG

I've asked you, Hanumig, not to bring my wife into our discussions.

HANUMIG

That's right. I forgot. We're not good enough to even mention your wife's name.

ARSHAG

Because I know you bring up her name to insult her or complain about her.

HANUMIG

We care about you. We don't say a thing about ninety-nine of our hundred complaints. And the one that we do mention, you seem to take as a personal insult.

ARSHAG

But my wife never complains about you at all.

MRS. DIROUHI

What could she possibly have to complain about? She has food, she has drink, she goes out—

ARSHAG

And you? Do you go hungry?

MRS. DIROUHI
My son, what kind of talk is that? Are you comparing us to her? All these years we've been your mother and sister! We deny ourselves, working and scrimping to keep up this house, for the good of the home. Now we have a stranger in our midst, so let's not act dishonorably in front of her. Let's make sure she is comfortable, has plenty to eat and drink, and can come and go freely, as she pleases. We've got our responsibilities and face them as best we can. *(Arshag shakes his head forcefully as his mother speaks.)*

ARSHAG
I give you a hundred sovereigns a month, Momma. You say you're denying yourselves. Tell me if you need more.

HANUMIG
Don't you see? With a fixed sum of money someone has got to deny herself if someone else is to spend lavishly.

ARSHAG
So: are you saying that the hundred sovereigns a month cover only my wife's expenses?

MRS. DIROUHI
Who else's then? Thank God *I* don't visits gardens, theaters and movies. *I* don't go to museums by car nor does *Hanumig.*

ARSHAG
But, Momma, why bring up movies and museums? Those are incidental expenses. I always pay for them separately. Tell me something: Do you live in this house with my wife? Eat at the same table? Have the same servants? Is your clothing made by the same tailors?

MRS. DIROUHI
We have all that because your wife has them. Before you got married we lived a simple life, as straight and narrow as the

36

road from Constantinople to this house in Pera. We didn't
have two servants then or custom-made clothes.

ARSHAG

That's true, but night and day you used to tell me it was
because we didn't have servants that no one asked for Hanumig's hand in marriage. And when you learned that I had
married a girl from a wealthy family, you started leading
the high life even before we moved into this richly furnished
house.

HANUMIG

Only so you wouldn't appear less in your wife's eyes.

ARSHAG

My wife is a plain girl. She doesn't care about such things.

MRS. DIROUHI

My poor boy, you're much too kind. She's got you believ-
ing her tastes are modest. Take away any one of her luxuries
and see what happens. Ask her to do a small household task
and see what she says.

ARSHAG

You say these things about Arousiag?

MRS. DIROUHI

You're so quick to take her side. Can't you see how she's
twisted your mind? Did you ever talk this way to us before?
Did you ever bring up things like accounts and money?
She makes you do these things. Shame on us. Shame on you
for going out of your way to hurt your poor sister's feelings.
We've proved ourselves true to you from your earliest years.
Now let's see what your wife is all about when she's put to a
test.

ARSHAG

(Aside) I didn't know what you were really like until this
moment! Now I know only too well what you're all about.

I see what games you're playing . . . . Just hold on, I'll play my own game with you. We'll see how you like it. *(Aloud, sweetly)* Mother, I'm amazed that you doubt the faith I have in you. Don't you realize that for a son the sweetest and dearest thing in the world is his mother, and for a brother his sister?

HANUMIG
(With bitterness) So you say.

ARSHAG
Look here, I'm going to prove how much I trust you, how much I need your love above all else. And I'm going to give you the chance to show again how much you love me.

HANUMIG
I've always made that clear and always will.

ARSHAG
Thank you, thank you very much. I really must have your complete devotion, now.

MRS. DIROUHI
Who but us could love you without reservation? A wife's love is selfish and put on. Your mother and sister are always yours. A wife can be yours today and someone else's tomorrow. You'll be convinced of that one day, Arshag. But I'm going to let you find out for yourself. I'm not going to say a word to you.

ARSHAG
(Seemingly agitated) No matter what, please don't desert me.

HANUMIG
We never will. We'll always stand by you.

ARSHAG
Even if I become poor and destitute—

HANUMIG

(Aside) What does he mean by that?

MRS. DIROUHI

(With a long suffering look) A mother never deserts her son.

HANUMIG

Or a sister her brother.

ARSHAG

Well then, I may as well tell you:—I've had a stroke of really bad luck—

HANUMIG

(Aside) I knew something was wrong the minute he came in! I hope he hasn't lost our money!

MRS. DIROUHI

What do you mean, my son? What's happened? Has your wife gotten involved in some sort of scandal?

ARSHAG

If she had, I'd have kicked her out of the house. It would all have been over. *(Mrs. Dirouhi and Hanumig signal to each other.)*

ARSHAG

This is very hard for me. But I must tell you because I need your help . . . . Mother, forgive me, forgive me. I'm bankrupt! I'm in debt up to my ears!

HANUMIG

Oh??! *(She turns away with a grim look.)*

MRS. DIROUHI

God have mercy on us! How could that be? What happened?

ARSHAG

I've been gambling!

MRS. DIROUHI
But you've never gambled in your whole life!

HANUMIG
I'm sure your wife is responsible. We can thank her for this.

ARSHAG
Business wasn't going well lately and I was having trouble covering the expenses of this house. I'd been dealing with a big customer for a while and all of a sudden he went bankrupt and that wrecked my own business. I had no way to make up the losses. Day after day, I had to find ways to pay off my creditors. And on top of that I had to find a hundred sovereigns for the house every month. There were the running expenses of the business, too. So to make money I took a chance at cards and won a thousand sovereigns in one hand. I was about to pull out of the game and move on. But I got greedy and careless. "I'll win back everything I lose," I said, and jumped into the water with all my clothes on. The more I played, the more I lost. The more I said, "I'll win," the more I lost. In the end, I was eight hundred sovereigns in the hole . . . . Now I don't know what I'm going to do—!

HANUMIG
Have you told your wife?

ARSHAG
Do you want her to know of my disgrace? Didn't you say just now that you didn't want to belittle me in her eyes when you spoke of upgrading the household help?

MRS. DIROUHI
How can we help you, now? I'll do everything in my power to help you, my son—!

HANUMIG
You don't have to tell your wife you lost money gambling. Just say you had a business setback. Let her worry about it.

She's enjoyed all the good times up to now; let her suffer the bad ones too.

MRS. DIROUHI
But we're going to suffer with her.

ARSHAG
Yes, and I'm truly sorry for you. We're going to have to let the servants go.

HANUMIG
(She wipes her eyes with a handkerchief.) I wish you had never gotten married.

MRS. DIROUHI
Your wife has brought this misfortune on us.

ARSHAG
She brought a dowry of three thousand sovereigns, too; don't forget that.

HANUMIG
What she brought, she spent. She'll have us living on a garbage dump next.

ARSHAG
You're right. We'll be sitting on a garbage dump if someone doesn't help us.

MRS. DIROUHI
If we could just think of a way to help you.

ARSHAG
Mother, can't we rent out our country house for five hundred sovereigns? That way I could pay off my gambling debts. Then we'll think of a way to save my business and my reputation, too. *(Hanumig sidles up to her mother, pulls on her sleeve, and shakes her head.)*

MRS. DIROUHI

I've set aside the income from that house for your sister so she'll always be able to support herself.

ARSHAG

I'll always be there to support her, Mother. Who's been looking after her all these years?

HANUMIG

You may have provided a bit of money, but we have taken care of the household and you. If you had rented rooms elsewhere, you would have had to pay for services. Remember when you came down with influenza? Who nursed you? Who washed your underwear? Who ironed your handkerchiefs? How quickly you forget!

ARSHAG

All right. We've helped one another. That's how it should be. I happen to be in a bad situation right now. When business picks up again, I'll cover all the expenses of the house again. Just don't embarrass me now, when I'm desperate.

MRS. DIROUHI

Let me give you a little advice. If you listen to it, you'll feel better. If you don't, I won't be responsible for what happens. Send your wife to her father's home for a little while, until we get straightened out and have time to think things over. You can turn to your relatives and friends for help. Someone will come through.

ARSHAG

I don't have any relatives closer than you. Where am I going to find closer friends than you? Mother, if you deny me, why should others help me?

HANUMIG

We're women. We can't meddle into business affairs.

SCENE 4

(Arousiag, Arshag, Hanumig, Mrs. Dirouhi)

AROUSIAG

Oh, Arshag, there you are.

ARSHAG

(Sadly) Hello—

AROUSIAG

What's the matter? Are you feeling ill?

ARSHAG

I've got . . . a . . . bad headache, yes.

AROUSIAG

(Upset) Let's call the doctor— *(Moves to ring the bell)*

ARSHAG

A doctor can't help me—

AROUSIAG

What's wrong with him, Momma? Hanumig? Everyone looks so sad. Tell me, what's wrong? Why do you make me repeat myself? Answer me—! *(Mrs. Dirouhi and Hanumig begin to cry.)*

ARSHAG

What good will it do to tell you? Hanumig says women are helpless. And you're a woman—

AROUSIAG

(She kneels before him and takes his hands.) What's the matter, Arshag? You must tell me. Are you tired? Are you worried about something? Are you in some sort of trouble?

HANUMIG

(Crying) Big trouble.

AROUSIAG

(Confused) All of you know something. Why do you keep it from me? Are you trying to drive me mad?

MRS. DIROUHI

He's lost all his money—

AROUSIAG

(Takes a deep breath and stands up) Is that the reason for all this gloom? Does a man get sick because of money, Arshag?

HANUMIG

It's going to affect the entire household—

AROUSIAG

So let it. We'll be together, Arshag. We'll work together and we'll fix everything.

ARSHAG

So you think it's that simple! Remember, tomorrow you'll be working in the kitchen. You'll have to scrub floors and wash clothes, Arousiag.

AROUSIAG

One doesn't cry because of things like that! Kitchen help and launderers are people just like us. I can do what they do—

MRS. DIROUHI

Of course! It's easy to boast. Talk is cheap! You'll have my son thinking you can really help. You can't even sweep a floor!

AROUSIAG

I can learn, Momma.

ARSHAG

There's more you should know. I need five hundred sovereigns to cover a debt of honor. I've got to have it by tonight.

And I don't even have five hundred shillings in my pocket!

AROUSIAG
What about my jewelry? It's worth at least five hundred sovereigns. Find someone right away and sell it to cover your debt. I'll go get it. *(Exits running)*

ARSHAG
You see, Mother? She really cares. Women can do something if they want to. You, both of you, have at least a thousand sovereigns worth of jewelry between you. But you can't bring yourselves to offer even one piece of it to help pay my debt. I even begged you to rent out the country house to help me. After all, half of it is mine legally. You denied me that, too. You heard Arousiag just now, what she's willing to do. She's gone to get all her valuables to help pull me through this crisis. How can you compare yourselves to her? I don't want anything from you. All I ask is that you treat her well and speak about her with respect.

MRS. DIROUHI
Your wife is mad. Respect her?! I've always worked for the good of the entire household—saving, budgeting and planning year after year. And I had you to care for and raise. I've always been proud of our good reputation. If I had spent carelessly all I owned, we'd have been out on the streets a long time ago. I didn't want to say this, but you've forced me to: How do you know your wife isn't flattering you for reasons of her own? Our motives are clear. Hers I'm not sure about!

ARSHAG
(Aside) What lies! *(Aloud)* Are you accusing my wife of something or other . . . without any proof of anything? You have no right to attack an innocent person. If you're angry with me, take it out on me!

MRS. DIROUHI
My son, a mother doesn't strike back at her son. I'm not angry with you, I don't want revenge! I just don't want to

see you walking around this house like a blind man. What I'm saying is: Open your eyes, see what's going on around you, try to take in, make sense of the things that are going on here! *(She exits angrily, followed by Hanumig, who gives her brother a fierce look.)*

SCENE 5
(Arshag, alone)

ARSHAG

I'm afraid I really have been blind to what's been going on in this house! What awful women!! They must have been hounding my wife from the very beginning. My sister glared at her with hatred in her eyes. And when I suggested renting out the country house Hanumig became vicious. Why, I've bought bonds for her with the rent money often in the past. They both must have plenty put away. And well over a thousand sovereigns in jewelry. And this other horrible, shameful secret I stumbled on . . . I can't believe it! It's destroying me. I'm shattered by the realization that both my mother and sister have duped me, cheated me in my own house. I wish I'd never found out! I've been blind all these years! I believed they were devoted to me, that they really loved me, were open and honest with me, yes I trusted their innocence, their quiet suffering womanhood—! I was lulled into feeling secure and happy with women who seemed to be thrifty homemakers . . . . What devil made me come home early today! I'd just gotten to the door of the house when I met someone from the Bank of Lyons right here on my doorstep, ringing my bell. I asked him what he wanted. He gave me a letter. It never occured to me for a moment that anyone beside myself had dealings with a bank! I didn't even look at the address, just assumed it was for me. So I opened the envelope. And what was it? Miss Hanumig Ardzatian's quarterly report which showed monthly deposits of twenty sovereigns at a time. I was shocked! Couldn't believe what I had read. I rushed upstairs to my mother's room to ask her about it. Luckily she wasn't there right then, but her account book, in Hanumig's handwriting, was on her desk. I wish I hadn't laid eyes on those accounts! Out of one hundred sovereigns a month I gave them, seventy went for the household expenses, ten they kept for their personal needs, and *twenty were deposited in the Bank of Lyons!* My mother was absolutely right! I've been walking around this house like a blind man! "Open your eyes, see what's going on around you—" I would have preferred to remain blind and ignorant rather than find out that my own mother is a thief. If she had come right out and asked me, I would have given her double the allowance rather than have her disgraced like this. *(Sits down for a moment and puts his head in his hands)* No, no— *(lifts his head)* my mother couldn't have planned a thing like this. Hanumig must have talked her into it. I remember how greedy she was when she was little. But then she seemed to change as she grew older, she seemed to grow pleasant and affectionate. We were close to each other then. She seemed the perfect sister in all respects. I got to love her dearly and looked after her welfare in every possible way. Only one thing I couldn't do: find her a husband. Was it my fault she couldn't find a man? Arousiag always said, "Let's make every effort to get the girl married." I never realized before how genuinely concerned my wife was about this family. At first I thought she'd be jealous of the other women in the house, in spite of her naturally gracious nature. How stupid of me to think that way even for a moment! I just didn't see clearly . . . . My poor wife. How she must have suffered with that monster around. I saw the hate and scorn in Hanumig's eyes when Arousiag went upstairs to get her jewelry for me. God, I wish I hadn't left the office early today! I wish I hadn't run into that bank clerk . . . I wish I hadn't read the bank statement! If I'd noticed the address on the envelope I certainly wouldn't have opened that letter. Hanumig would have lied about it and I would have believed her. Who knows how many lies she's told me all through the years! I used to feel safe and carefree in my own house, until I made the mistake of opening someone else's mail! Yes, she's guilty all right! But aren't we all guilty of something or other? And then, the second mistake of looking

47

into my mother's account book. I've never done that before. And then the third mistake: to say I was bankrupt and in debt. How am I going to free myself from all these lies? Once a man gets caught in a web of this kind, he gets more and more involved. When you fall into quicksand, you sink deeper and deeper with every step. What am I going to say to Arousiag? I'd rather die than tell her my mother and my sister are frauds. But how else can I explain why I lied about being bankrupt and in debt? I just can't do it! I've got to keep lying. Follow my mother's advice. I've got to open my eyes and look around me. Not because I suspect Arousiag of anything, but to find out how my mother and sister get on with my wife in my absence. I know what I'll do: when Arousiag brings me her valuables, I'll take them and pretend to go out. Instead I'll hide close by so that I can see and hear everything with my own eyes and ears.

SCENE 6
(Arousiag and Arshag)

AROUSIAG
(Enters breathlessly, carrying a box) Arshag, Arshag, it's all in here. I had a little money and put that in the box too. Here, take it quickly, sell it, go on. And please don't get so worked up again, as you did before. I thought you were sick. You frightened me.

ARSHAG
Arousiag, I can't take your jewelry. You've only had these a year or two and have hardly worn them. Someone young like you should have such things to wear at parties, to look dazzling. I don't want you to look dull while your friends sparkle. You always look so handsome wearing them.

AROUSIAG
(Shakes her finger to chide him) Liar! Didn't you tell me that my necklace hid the beauty of my neck and that my arms looked more attractive without bracelets and that rings

48

took away from the daintiness of my fingers? Were you just flattering me when you said all those things?

ARSHAG
Arousiag, I know how important jewelry is to a woman. It may not be her whole life but it's a good part of it, the key to her happiness . . . . No, no, Arousiag, I can't let you give it up. I'll find another way to solve my problem. Put them back, go on.

AROUSIAG
Don't be silly, Arshag. You're treating me like a simple-minded ninny who thinks that precious stones and metals are the most important things in a woman's life. Why keep them locked up in a box? I use them maybe twice a year. Is that worth all the suffering you're going through? I'd give my blood, my very life to help you. So take these, all of them, and sell them to pay off your debts so we can be at peace again. Then we'll write to my father. He'll help you.

ARSHAG
No, you mustn't! Don't write to your father. These will cover everything. Thanks, Arousiag. You're really very special, one of a kind, my guardian angel. Why should I worry about a thing, suffer alone when I have a heart like yours next to mine? Yes, I'll go right away and put an end to all this. I'll find out exactly how much I owe and pay up. But you must promise me you won't write a word about this to your father. I don't want anyone out there to know about my troubles. I'll find a way out of the difficulty in my own way. Quietly. I'll get out of it, my love, rest assured.

AROUSIAG
I'll do whatever you think is best—

ARSHAG
Then listen. I won't be back for dinner this evening. I may not be through until well past midnight, so don't wait up for me. Let the servants go to bed. Put out all the lights except

for the lamp in this room. I'll have something to eat outside, so when I get back I can get right to work here, in this room.

AROUSIAG

All right. Don't worry about us. Just take care of yourself. It's grown a bit chilly. Put on your coat and give me a kiss. *(They embrace.)* Good luck—!

SCENE 7
(Arousiag, alone)

AROUSIAG

(A servant enters, lights the lamps and goes out.) I finally calmed him down and sent him off in a good mood. I'm glad I thought of the jewelry. What else was there? I wish I had had more to give him. Will he be able to settle everything with so little? If not, we'll just have to learn to live more economically. I really don't care. We live in tasteless luxury here. These gilded pieces are nothing special; you can find them in any shop. There's nothing I really like about this house except my own room, where I have my pictures, my souvenirs and keepsakes and the other things I treasure. They remind me of my family and the wonderful times we had together years ago. I would really have preferred a small apartment of my own, arranged the way I like, with lots of plants and flowers all around. I'm supposed to be worried about ending up in the kitchen—to me it would be a pleasure if I could be with Arshag, just the two of us, without any harsh critics pouncing on me all the time. I'd cook the meals for my husband with my own hands, set the table for him, wait on him in every way. I'd give him all my attention. If only things could be like that, being poor wouldn't frighten me one bit. There's even something romantic about struggling for the one you love. The only trouble is that Momma and Hanumig will be very unhappy. They live to keep up appearances. And they'll suffer if others see them poor. They would rather die than see their home, furniture and servants taken away from them. They would be miserable and make us mis-

erable with them. So we must try to borrow money. But how —if Arshag won't let me write to my father? He said it very clearly not to write to him. *(She paces up and down the room talking to herself from time to time.)* I've got to find a way to solve this problem! *(Puts her hands to her forehead)* Yes, that might work. I'll write to Zareh; he'll know what to do. Tomorrow I'll take the letter to the post office and mail it myself . . . . It'll be my secret—! In a few days I'll have some money in hand . . . . We'll be safe. *(A bell rings.)* There's the dinner bell. I really don't have any appetite for food or talk this evening!

SCENE 8
(Servant, Arousiag)

SERVANT
Madam, dinner is served.

AROUSIAG
Are Mother and Miss Hanumig coming?

SERVANT
Miss Hanumig won't be at dinner. She's indisposed. Mrs. Ardzatian is already sitting down.

AROUSIAG
I'll be right there. *(Exits, followed by Servant)*

SCENE 9
(Hanumig, alone)

HANUMIG
(She tiptoes into the empty room stealthily, like a thief.) We'll be ruined! Lose everything we've got! We'll be poor! How could my luck turn like this! I remember when we lived in a plain house and had ordinary friends. Mother did the cooking. My aunt did all the house work. We lived modestly.

51

Then my brother's business began to improve. We got rid of my aunt and hired a maid. We were doing well when my brother's work took him to Smyrna. He met the daughter of a rich businessman and married her. We were afraid he would stay on there and leave us stranded here without any means of support. We wrote one letter after another. And like it or not, we had to plead with his wife to have my brother bring her here. I wrote the letter myself. I wish I had broken my hand before writing! And even before they got here, my brother sent us money to move to Pera, on this elegant street, and we rented this large house with all these fine pieces of furniture. We rented out our old house in the country and I banked the rent money for myself. We hired two servants, a secretary and a butler all in full uniform. We had everything. All our rich neighbors come to call. Of course we maintain a respectful distance, so that we don't give the impression of peasants who haven't seen the world. There never was a day I went out alone; always with Mother and very often took the carriage. If things had gone on that way— I would certainly have made a good marriage by this time. Everyone admired me. What a lovely girl, gracious, respectable, everyone said. But my happiness didn't last very long. My brother took his wife to Europe for three months before coming here. No sooner did his bride step through that door than our luck changed. I wish she had broken her legs coming here, never entered this house. She took over everything. Now she's the one they all flock around, all the respect and honor go to her. Everywhere we go, she's the center of attraction. They offer everything first to her, serve her first because she throws herself at people, that bitch! And here *I* am, carrying on our gracious style of living, dressing always in sober colors, looking straight ahead when out walking, never getting involved in idle conversations, genteel in all things—behaving as all young well-brought up girls should. That one, instead, shows no reserve at all! She wears bright dresses, low cut blouses, bouquets pinned to her breast. What more can I say? And my brother doesn't say a word to her! At first, we kept quiet because she *is* the daughter of a rich businessman. We let her do what she wanted. But then we

52

realized that we were spoiling her. We began to remind her of her faults and tried to force her to change. I had almost won back my advantage, almost had the run of the house again, and Mother was getting ready to talk to Arshag about his wife's intolerable behavior, when suddenly misfortune struck! What's left to say when one has had bad luck all through life and things get turned upside down—? Now I've got to fend for myself. They're sure to start selling everything in a day or so. Arshag doesn't know everything we have. And we've told Arousiag all along that everything in this house belongs to us . . . . I'll just start collecting a few things and take them to my room so we can get to keep something. *(She takes out a key from her pocket, opens a closet, takes several pieces of silver plate and puts them to one side. Footsteps can be heard approaching.)* Someone's coming! It's Arousiag. I'd better leave. *(She pushes the silver to one side on the floor and hurries off.)*

SCENE 10
(Arousiag, alone)

AROUSIAG

(She enters carrying a writing case and inkstand.) Mother and Hanumig must be in their rooms. I told the servants to go to bed. I'll wait here for Arshag, so I can open the door for him myself when he comes. I won't be able to sleep until he's home. I wonder if he'll make it! Who knows what trouble he's going through this very minute, my poor Arshag! Custom and tradition are really strange things. A man works his head off, struggles to make a living while we three women are comfortably settled here at home, without a care, and sleep soundly at night. *Why?* That's the *custom!* How absurd! Custom! Arshag should have stayed home to rest tonight and *we* should have gone out instead, and found ways to help ourselves. But what can I do on my own? My hands are tied. I can't do anything without . . . permission . . . . No, I *must* write this letter! But I don't want Mother and Hanumig to find out. They'd string me up and hang me if they knew.

53

(She sits at the writing table, facing the audience, and begins to write.)

SCENE 11
(Arshag, Arousiag)

ARSHAG
(Speaking to himself) The commandment is clear. Honor thy mother. Blessed is the son who does so. "Open your eyes," she said. If I hadn't, how would I have found out that there's a thief in my home and that thief—I'm sorry to say—is my own sister. All very sad, very sad—but let her take what she wants and leave. She can have the silver, the gold, all the valuables I own. I don't care. But I don't know how I will bring myself to look her in the eye let alone talk to her. Oh, she's used to this. She's absolutely without shame. She'll probably accuse someone else . . . . I've got to put an end to this disgraceful episode. I've got to tell her I know everything. Yes, I'll take these things and hide them. She'll try to find them. Let's see what happens . . . . *(He picks up the silver and carries it out of the room.)*

SCENE 12
(Hanumig, Arousiag)

HANUMIG
(She tiptoes in, looks around for the silver without success, grows confused, then frustrated and angry as she approaches Arousiag with a menacing look, muttering all the while to herself.) You, you . . . you . . . thief! I've caught you! I've caught you red-handed! I've got you all right!

AROUSIAG
(She doesn't see her.) There, I've managed to finish this letter before Arshag returns. I was afraid he'd catch me at it. *(She takes out an envelope and addresses it, speaking out loud as she writes the words.)* Monsieur Zareh Tatosian, Smyrna.

(She places the letter in it and seals the envelope.)

HANUMIG
(Comes up close) I caught you!!!

AROUSIAG
(Startled, standing) You frightened me, Hanumig. *(She takes the envelope from the table and puts it in her pocket.)*

HANUMIG
What are you afraid of? I don't eat up people! "Courage in a thief doesn't last long." Isn't that true?

AROUSIAG
(Annoyed) I don't know what you're talking about—

HANUMIG
No, you don't know anything! Why should you know anything? You thought I was asleep! You never dreamed I'd be right here in this room! . . . If guilt were a sable coat, no one would want to wear it! All right! I'll spell it out for you: Where did you put the silver? What happened to the silver?

AROUSIAG
(Calm now, cold) How would *I* know—?

HANUMIG
(Shouts) You're going to return that silver right now, *now!* If you don't, I'll shout and scream and wake up everybody. I'll call the servants. I'll disgrace you in front of everyone!

AROUSIAG
You're raving, Hanumig! What have I got to do with your silver? Look for it where *you* put it—

HANUMIG
I put the pieces right there, here on the floor, next to the closet. I was going . . . to polish them, but Mother called and I left them and ran upstairs. And now I come back to find

55

them stolen!

AROUSIAG

Who would steal them? You've probably forgotten where
you put them.

HANUMIG

I'm not like you, I don't forget where I put things! You're
not going to fool me with that kind of talk! Bring out the
silver or I'll bring out something else! *(Arshag appears on the
threshhold.)*

SCENE 13
(Arousiag, Hanumig, Arshag)

AROUSIAG

(Doesn't see Arshag) You're very confused tonight, dear sister. I don't want to hurt your feelings, but I certainly can't
help you. I haven't laid eyes on the silver!

HANUMIG
(Runs at her, yelling) Where is it? Where is the silver?

ARSHAG

(He comes forward slowly, calmly, the silver in his hands.)
Here it is. And I've been here too, for an hour. I saw a thief
come in, open the closet, take out the silver, start to carry it
off, and then, hearing footsteps, drop everything to the floor
and run off. I picked up the silver and hid it. *(Mrs. Dirouhi
enters after a few seconds of silence.)*

SCENE 14
(Mrs. Dirouhi, Arousiag, Arshag, Hanumig)

MRS. DIROUHI

What is all this! A thief! In my house? What else can possibly
happen to us! Arousiag, you must have left the window

in this room open again.

AROUSIAG
Did you see who it was, Arshag? Couldn't you catch the thief?

ARSHAG
I saw who it was with my own eyes, Arousiag, but I was so ashamed I could not stop it.

HANUMIG
You were imagining things. There's no thief here. I took the silver from the closet to clean and polish. I couldn't sleep so I came down to take it up to my room. But if you want to catch someone at something, ask your wife what is in the envelope she hid in her pocket when she saw me.

AROUSIAG
I don't know what the thief and the robbery have to do with the envelope. You seem very confused tonight, Hanumig.

HANUMIG
Why not let us see the envelope so we can tell whether I'm confused or not! What's there to hide?

MRS. DIROUHI
I won't have secrets in my house! Secrets are evil.

AROUSIAG
And what if I've hidden something good?

MRS. DIROUHI
Good or bad, I must know what you're hiding.

ARSHAG
You have no right, Mother. My wife's secret is her own.

MRS. DIROUHI
Arshag, my son. What did I tell you a little while ago? Open

your eyes. Look around you. Obviously I have some reason for suspicion or I wouldn't speak this way. How do I know what's going on in this house? You leave in the morning and are away all day. Your wife goes to her room and writes. What is she writing, writing all the time?

ARSHAG
Mother, she's writing a novel.

HANUMIG
So tell me, is that the novel in her pocket?

AROUSIAG
No, what's in my pocket is not a novel. It's a letter. But . . . please don't ask me to show it to you.

HANUMIG
I knew all along you wouldn't dare show it!

ARSHAG
Please, Arousiag, let them have it and put an end to all this suspicion.

AROUSIAG
So, they really *do* suspect me of something!

HANUMIG
If you want to put it that way, yes! We have our suspicions about you!

AROUSIAG
Well then, take it. (*She pulls out the letter and throws it on the table.*)

HANUMIG
(*She seizes it, reads the name and address out loud.*) Monsieur Zareh Tatosian, Smyrna. (*Triumphant*) Now! Do you understand, brother?

MRS. DIROUHI

(Strikes her head with both hands) Oh, my poor poor boy—!

HANUMIG

A disgrace, that's what it is! *(She hides her face in her hands, while Arousiag smiles, her arms crossed at her breast.)*

ARSHAG

(Extracts the letter from the envelope and reads out loud) "My dear cousin. I beg you, if you can, without any delay, to pass the enclosed letter to my mother and to please keep it from my father. I would consider this a great favor for which I shall be most grateful." *(To his mother and sister)* Well, what have you got to say?

AROUSIAG

Don't bother reading the letter to my mother. Here, Arshag, let me have it—

HANUMIG

No! The first letter is obviously a cover. It has no purpose. The secret is the other letter. Go on, read it if you dare.

ARSHAG

(Reads) "Dear Mother, you always said I should turn to you when I needed help. I am following your wish in writing to you now. But you need not worry. I have no problems and you musn't be uneasy. Actually, I have a very good life here. You know how much I love my Arshag and he loves me. I couldn't ask for more in this world. The trouble has to do with material concerns. I need some money to help out someone, but I don't want either my husband or father to know about it. I'm sure you will approve of what I'm doing once you learn about it. I need a few hundred pieces of gold. Please, I beg you, send me what you can quickly and you'll make your only daughter very happy." *(He throws the letter on the table, extends his arms and embraces his wife while Mrs. Dirouhi and Hanumig keep their heads down in shame.)*

CURTAIN

AFTERWORD

On the stage of current "feminist" and "liberation" causes, in which claims are often voiced aggressively for effect and immediate action, *The Bride* may appear bland and perhaps even old-fashioned. But for those who grasp the value of historical evolution in such matters, the play is not only an interesting point of departure, a beginning of awareness of women as individuals who are sharply sensitive to the need to mold relationships and values in their own terms but, for its time, a bold statement too. If we approach such a work with contemporary attitudes alone, we lose both the value of the play within the large feminist "statement" as it has come to be articulated through several decades and the special flavor of the place and time in which it was written.

In certain respects, *The Bride* reflects the role of women, generally, at the end of the nineteenth century. In Anatolia and Constantinople, as in other parts of the world at that time, women were expected to live within a rigorously limited environment, a house- and family-oriented structure where marriage and children were the only respectable and desirable ends. Women were expected to be modest, retiring, subdued in dress, speech and manners generally. Their voice carried no authority; their accomplishments were the efficient handling of servants, embroidery, sewing, and carefully restricted public appearances in which they were expected to follow certain rules of social behavior.

But *The Bride*—like the exotic foods we all enjoy in our cosmopolitan environment—has a taste of its own, a color and shape determined by Armenian society of the time. The new wife went to live with her husband's family and took a secondary place there—his sisters and mother having precedence over her. In all things, the Armenian bride was expected to obey not just her husband but his mother and sisters as well. Whatever her assets, only one counted ultimately to determine how others would treat her in her husband's household, where the mother-in-law rules: her dowry. Arousiag—the young bride in this play—has come

60

with an impressive wedding gift (her father is very wealthy). But this fact doesn't ingratiate her with her sister-in-law and mother-in-law. On the contrary, they seem bent on finding fault with her, humiliating her, proving her flighty and immodest. Her dowry provokes the unmarried sister-in-law's envy and hatred—since Hanumig has not yet been successful in attracting a suitor. Ideally, Arshag should have married his sister off before taking a wife himself. In this and other ways, Zabel Asadour—the woman playwright and journalist, author of *The Bride*—puts the excesses of her society to a subtle test.

Subtle, for the basic premises are in no way ever undermined. In her Armenian setting and within the special set of rigorous social and private circumstances which prevailed at the time, Asadour deftly portrays the young Arousiag trying to find her bearings in her husband's house. Trapped by the jealousy of her sister-in-law, the formal demands of her mother-in-law, the rigid way of life they insist upon, the young bride learns to be cheerful in the face of veiled accusations and insults and never complains to her husband. She is sustained by his complete devotion to her; and we are reminded in many ways that theirs is a marriage of love (something contrary to all propriety). The fact that her substantial dowry has enabled the family to move from the country to the city and assume all the elegant trappings of their well-off neighbors doesn't mitigate the circumstances: Arousiag is the intruder who is making waves, who seems to outshine everyone, including and especially the unmarried sister-in-law, Hanumig.

What is especially provocative about this play as a "feminist" statement is the battle of wits it dramatizes. Of course, women, in all ages, always have found their way through the confining restrictions imposed on them; and plays like Goldoni's *Mistress of the Inn*, Shakespeare's *The Taming of the Shrew*, Strindberg's *Miss Julie* even, like *The Bride*, dramatize that truth impressively. Ostensibly rooted in the shadows of stultifying tradition and customs, such women apply their talents to shifting the pressure points, eroding unobtrusively the demands made upon them and bringing their own values to bear.

In the midst of hypocrisy and blatant vulgarities, Arousiag is a bright presence, a shining example of good-natured openness. She applies her talents to working within a seemingly impossible set of values, finding her way through the intrigues created by her husband's family. In today's direct approach to such matters, Arousiag's tactics may seem at best half-measures. But in its basic insistence on bringing into play all the weapons and strategy at one's command, *The Bride* commands attention. It is, in fact, a complex statement of how shrewd maneuvering can work in two directions at once and in contradictory ways—for both ill and good. Hanumig, the envious greedy and selfcentered sister-in-law, whose hypocritical behavior follows the accepted norms (at least superficially) uses all her skills and native cunning to look after her interests, and seems to have succeeded. Only an accident brings her thefts to light. Arousiag, the bride, has her own secrets to keep, her own cunning to enlist if the honor of the family is to be preserved. We watch both these women use their native talents to ward off what they consider to be defeat and humiliation. And if Arousiag wins out it is not only because her cause is a better one, but also because her manner is consistently open and good-natured. She has no malice in her: she may have secrets to keep but nothing to hide.

In this context, the play takes on a vivid clarity of purpose that should appeal to all those who espouse the feminist cause. The women respond to crises (whether or not such crises are valid or sound does not really matter here) with all their talents. Their native qualities are reinforced by the need to press their claims within the established restrictions: Arousiag will never talk back to her husband or speak against his family; Hanumig will never say openly what it is that gnaws at her or confess to her personal greed and envy. The crises bring out the best and worst in the two women. To preserve themselves within the social bonds they cannot escape, they must find their true stride and use all their energies in a way that does not jolt reality. Of course, in Hanumig's case reality *is* shattered with the knowledge of her thefts—the money she has diverted from her brother's account into a secret one of her own, and the silver pieces she has stowed away to hide and keep for herself before the house and all its belongings are sold to pay Arshag's debts.

Structurally, the play has certain flaws—the ending, for example, is much too abrupt. Moreover, there are at times passages and speeches of unrelieved moralistic fervor and blatant unethical intentions. Still, given the time and place, such "monologues" serve a purpose. *The Bride* is, after all, a "first" in every way, and its author perfectly aware of the difficulties of asserting herself on behalf of women in a "closed" society. That she was able to provide a statement for the cause of women, finding the delicate balance and a certain dramatic "distance" to insure the success of her effort is testimony to her talent as a writer and her strength as a woman sure of herself and her special role.

ANNE PAOLUCCI
(President, Council on National Literatures)

THE CRITICS

Nishan Parlakian's translation of Zabel Asadour's *The Bride* is a milestone in the literature of women's causes and excellent reading! It is also a most welcome addition to Armenian texts in translation.

MARIO FRATTI *(Playwright and Drama Critic, Adaptor of Tony-Award-Winning Musical NINE)*

An extraordinary play. An historically-important feminist work, witty as well. This talented Armenian playwright has not only crafted a vivid illustration of her time, but also given us an eloquent universal statement on human right.

PATRICK COLLINS *(WNYC-TV)*

Comic elements blend with dramatic realities in this entertaining romantic treatment of a loving and loyal wife who finds the way to uncover the greedy possessiveness and hypocrisy of her in-laws. We have here all the major elements and concoctions for a marvelous Mozart- or Rossini-style comic opera (Menotti: please note!)—

JOSEPH KING *(Drama Critic, L. I. INDEPENDENT VOICE, Member of New York Outer Critics Circle)*

The Bride is a forceful statement about the ideal role of women within an established tradition. Zabel Asadour was one of the first modern feminists but not in an outspoken sense; she remained always true to her own inner self, her honest sensibility. Nishan Parlakian has produced a forceful and eminently readable text in English. He has done it again!

SHOGHERE MARKARIAN *(Writer and Critic)*

Parlakian has infused his translation of this memorable Armenian play with his own intuitive theatricality, anticipating as it does the liberated woman of today.

MAURICE EDWARDS *(Artistic Director, The Classic Theatre)*

Another gem has been added to the Armenian repertory in English, thanks to the inimitable skill of Nishan Parlakian . . . .

(From the publisher's "Book News")